BIRTHING AGE

poems by

Joan Barasovska

Finishing Line Press
Georgetown, Kentucky

BIRTHING AGE

*For Frankie Rubinstein,
the best teacher,
on her 100th*

One day, one day, one day, this one day.
Betty Adcock

Copyright © 2018 by Joan Barasovska
ISBN 978-1-63534-705-0 First Edition
All rights reserved under International and Pan-American Copyright Conventions. No part of this book may be reproduced in any manner whatsoever without written permission from the publisher, except in the case of brief quotations embodied in critical articles and reviews.

ACKNOWLEDGMENTS

"High Relief" appeared in *Sing, Heavenly Muse* (1977)
"October" appeared in the 2013 edition of *Pinesong*, the North Carolina Poetry Society's awards anthology.
"Early March" was selected by Poetry in Plain Sight for one of its April, 2017, posters.
"Bathing Mama" won honorable mention in the 2015 Flyleaf Books Poetry Contest
"Birthing Age" appeared in *A Gathering of Poets* (Jacar Press, 2016)

I am grateful to The Poet Fools, my critique group, for their encouragement, advice, and honesty. As is our custom, I will simply say, "Thank you for your helpful comments."

Charlotte Weiser Pamplin's astonishing daffodil photograph on the cover makes this book visually alive. I believe that her photograph of the author demonstrates our friendship.

My eternal gratitude goes to my first best reader, Pam Baggett, friend extraordinaire and extraordinary poet.

Publisher: Leah Maines
Editor: Christen Kincaid
Cover Art: Charlotte Weiser Pamplin
Author Photo: Charlotte Weiser Pamplin
Cover Design: Elizabeth Maines McCleavy

Printed in the USA on acid-free paper.
Order online: www.finishinglinepress.com
also available on amazon.com

Author inquiries and mail orders:
Finishing Line Press
P. O. Box 1626
Georgetown, Kentucky 40324
U. S. A.

Table of Contents

So Young

Flight 1
My Father Teaches Me to Dive 2
No One Knows About This 4
The Day I Walked on Fire 5
Pine Street 6
High Relief 7

The Big Story

The Thousand Things 8
Week at the Beach 9
Crossroad Blues 10
On a Dark Road in Winter 11
Divorce 12
Neat Trick 13
Crossing 14
Home 15
Lucky 16
Without a Kiss 17
What I Did Wrong 18

Turning

Late September 19
October 20
Let Winter Come 21
First Dawn in Snowland 22
Early March 23
Dogwood 24
Summer's Start 25
Summer 26

Birthing Age

Elizabeth Nax 27
Bathing Mama 28
Down to a Point 29
World 30
Birthing Age 31

SO YOUNG

Flight

Locust Twenty-Second St. James Twenty-Third then Locust again
over and over on my blue Schwinn until the streetlights come on
which is earlier in September and you come in earlier for your bath
but the air's still hot and wet and dirty but not for me I fly
over sheets of slate bump over cracks break your mother's back
on my three-speed bike pigtails flying in our own wind
and we reach speed as the lights come on and we take
the giant sycamore on Locust Street high into the night
into the yellow buzzing light clear up to the fat orange moon

My Father Teaches Me to Dive

I am nine.
I stand straight
and curl my toes tight
around the pool's edge.
We're at the deep end.
Kids splash and yell
way off in the shallow end,
cordoned off by a rope
strung with red buoys.

Two low boards flank
The High Dive:
its metal ladder,
up and up,
the narrow board,
the spring I hear
each time someone
flies off.

But first I have to learn.
I wear my hand-me-down
bathing suit, tight rubber cap.
Daddy wears plaid trunks.
He crouches next to me
to tell me what to do.
Tuck chin, curl over,
arms straight down,
hands in prayer
pointed to the water.
Toes curled, belly sucked in,
his arm stretched across my shins
to guide me up and over.
He says, "Up and over!"

Perfect form,
the perfect swan of me,
darts and parts the water!
I stream away as far
as breath will last
to make him laugh
when I pop up
and gasp.

No One Knows About This

At night the trees lie down to rest.
They unclench their roots, groan,
and all sink down.
It makes a dry, rough sound.
They face the moon.
Their twigs sometimes break off,
the older branches don't.
They mesh with other trees
in a high, dense stack.
At sunrise they rustle,
yank themselves upright.
Some leaves get lost.
They twist to get the angle right
and dig in for the day.

The Day I Walked on Fire

it wasn't fire
it was ginkgo leaves
the sun lit them yellow
they were juicy with heat

the day I walked on ginkgo leaves
I imagined they were fire
that my shoes were melting
that my feet were burning

and I felt no pain
on that autumn day
when I burned to be
a holy woman

Pine Street

a woman walks
spinning a line
of sight
jarred by her pace

a woman who
carries her mind
in her gaze
life in her body

a woman walks
passing windows
into lives
she may step inside

a woman's gait
her quick steps
streets she takes
knowing her way

her traveling mind
a woman in flight
she sees into trees
follows their rise

she studies the work
of her breath
inside a woman
walking outside

High Relief

it is the figure of a woman running
asleep on her side
the outline of a runner
with knees raised and slanted back
a woman pinched up like salt and dropped
onto the bed to run into her dreams
whose sleeping leaded form
embossed upon the bed is a medal
a coin struck by the race of women
whose sleep is a sprint

THE BIG STORY

The Thousand Things

It's eight o'clock.
You have nursed the baby to sleep, but he will wake in the night.
You have read and sung his sister to bed.
The house waits to be made.
The man reads in his study, floating lightly above the world.

You begin.
From room to room to room you pick up toys, cups, trucks,
the tiny, tiny things the homemaker sees.
You spread order from room to room to room.
The wash churns in its machines,
the dinner plates click against the pots.
You pack her lunch, you sign permission slips,
you sweep the kitchen into a plastic pan.

There's Zen in the swinging rhythm of your broom,
but it's just monotony, as sure as dust, and daily.
You sponge the counters to a shine.
You take the trash out, mash down the stinking bags,
drag the can to the crumbling curb.
He's writing now.

The thousand things will be there for you
for a thousand thousand nights,
and he'll be sitting in his chair.

Week at the Beach

When the family went to the beach,
the two children, he, aloof, content to wander,
myself, laundress, cook, there to sweep sand,
slather sunscreen on little arms and backs, then soap it off,
the kids and I, splashing in shallow, friendly waves,
would watch him disappear far off, out to the beckoning sea.
The kids, so worried: *Where is Daddy?*
When will he come back? I can't see him anymore!
I contemplated single motherhood,
the generous life insurance policy,
same chores, of course, but a lighter burden,
one less big mouth to feed, big plate to load.
His mother and the kids would be devastated,
but not I.

Crossroad Blues

Soul in a cracked leather satchel,
Robert Johnson strode, near midnight,
to crossed roads in the Delta dark.
Lucifer was cooling his heels,
waiting for the deal to go down.

Satchel handed over,
The Dark One scratched a cross on Johnson's throat.
Until his murder at twenty-seven,
Johnson poured molten blues
across Mississippi.

My own blues' coordinates confound me.
At the crossroads of morning I might wake
golden or struck down by The Dark One,
my heart ashen in my lap,
no compass, no map.

When I pass this way, midnight on my brow,
know that I'm traveling blind.
Walk on by, Devil.
It could be years before
I see a road out.

On a Dark Road in Winter

I am driving on, faster, faster
traveling alone
two lights ahead, two behind
woods at each side
I will not pass this way again

don't lead me, don't follow
roads lead to other roads
you will never see
I speed forward with blind certainty
I am leaving you, heading away

Divorce

In the shtetl of my heart I hoed weeds in rows
of cabbages and potatoes. Mud crusted the hem
of my black wool skirt. I stoked an iron stove
to boil the thin peasant soup that fed my family.
Daily, I tied a faded babushka under my chin.
I muttered curses on the Tsar's head and wished
him dead. In the village of my marriage
I hid kopeks in a twisted rag, tokens of my rage.
At last, by moonlight, I trudged miles,
footsore in worn boots, to book passage
in steerage across waters I had never seen.
A lifted lamp waited by the foreign shore.

Neat Trick

to flip my skin inside-out
damp pearly raw
to the bruised world

it's a love trick
flick of the wrist
with a potato peeler

perfect flesh
pressed to the heart
where it doesn't belong

all wrong
walking the world
like a flayed thing

no seams
no stitches
no ring

Crossing

The tall woman in my headlights had her back to me.
I saw her light shirt, dark pants, dark skin.
She was crossing a black two-lane road on a black night, not looking.
There was trouble, she was in the wrong place, she wasn't young,
I didn't see her face.

I was nearly home.
The road curved and straightened in its familiar way.
There are women who have no home at all,
who shelter in the woods and blunder onto dark roads blindly.

I have been blind and crossed against the light.
I have yearned for safe passage to some other side.
Trouble has chased me into the path of worse trouble,
the heedless dash, the headlong flight
that smashes everything around it.

My headlights found my house waiting, one light on.
I have the key.
That woman in the road had passed into the night.

Home

This is the temple of my adult aloneness.   ~David Whyte

I know my way there in the dark, in fog and rain and early light.
The broad gray house is hidden in this winter's woods.
I look out upon the sloping land, the distant road.
High above the fireplace a painting hangs, a single longleaf pine,
extravagant and endangered.

The narrow years are over.
This glass door opens upon my bright domain,
a house for long dreams, the tower of my remaining days.
I am no longer wanting for direction, or rest, or peace.
This brightness shall shroud my living and shelter my last sleep.

I walk from room to room.
I ring the doorbell
and I'm the one who's home.

Lucky

This is the late making of a self
after three decades in a man's slipstream,
and it takes imagination to know it's best,
this hard way, this coming-home-alone way,
now that I'm making my own luck
with just three leaves on a stem of clover,
over the front door a bent rusty horseshoe,
and it's the fact of ordinary quiet, ordinary sleep,
that astounds me with relief
that I was strong enough to break away
and take my chances.

Without a Kiss

When she was Sleeping Beauty,
lying in a swoon in the bramble forest,
he told her she was beautiful,
her Ruler, her Wolf Prince.

When she was Sleeping Beauty,
scrubbing floors and boiling beans,
he told her to dress in royal raiment
but all she wore was rags.

When she was Sleeping Beauty,
in a blind trance for thirty years,
he told her what to do and say
but all she did and said was wrong.

When she was Sleeping Beauty,
bearing her liege's beautiful children,
he told her he was lonely
but she had ceased to care.

When she awoke, without a kiss,
and parted the bramble thicket,
The Old King shouted and raged
but Beauty had slipped away.

What I Did Wrong

walked out
nowhere to go
cursed the past
cursed the man
drove 60
on the wrong roads
left home
60 years old

what I did right
was what I did wrong
left the past
just in time
sped up improvised
cursed my fears
found safe ground
wrote this down

TURNING

Late September

Morning chill, darker still each day as fall skims light
from summer's plenitude. Summer's glut hangs on
in muggy days, leaves merged in massed and varied greens.
The chill is coming, the brightness trees
will wear until their light release of leaves.
The turn we take each year compels our vision forward,
then inward toward the lengthening, darkening past.

October
> *Oh Lord, how shining and festive is your gift to us, if we only look, and see.* ~Mary Oliver

See how the roads fill overnight with fallen leaves
and are blown clean by early morning.
A tang in the air I taste, and the chill there.
I have walked these roads in summer and in spring,
in the steam of Carolina and its blossoming,
I have crunched a skin of frost beneath my boots –
but first, this ripening.
The chilling into winter begins with this,
this brightening.

Let Winter Come
    after "Let Evening Come" by Jane Kenyon

The sun at noon is weak,
the day draws in short,
night creeps in the woods.

Let winter chase small creatures into hiding,
starve those too weak to forage,
draw us indoors seeking the light we crave.

Ice stiffens creeks and ditches,
frozen rain silvers every twig,
glasses pebbles, topples patient trees.

The tilt of Earth leaves us bereft
when winter starts its work
of pitiless conclusion.

Let the great cold come and pass.
What lasts lives on to spring,
'til spring lets summer in.

First Dawn in Snowland

A seamless cover, undulant, clean,
smooths every ragged edge below.
Faint tracks, rabbit, deer,
sunk as if by deliberate design,
trace paths in spreads of bluish-white.
Wet trees, black bark,
steel-cold rocks dotted down the hill.
All is still, soundless,
stunned into a frozen scene,
dawn rising on a fitful night,
tucking it in bed between cool sheets.

Early March

How I love daffodils,
so brave, bright, reckless,
bent by February storms,
trusting March
to stand them up again.
I have kept my childish faith in spring,
daffodils by the roadside,
cold rains that smash,
kind days that tip
the tender faces up,
and hidden underground,
the secret store
of next year's daffodils.

Dogwood

its pale serrated faces
opened out too early
everything budded early
pear daffodil tulip cherry

rough bark   brief flowering
my mother's favorite tree
hers was a bitter heart
mine ripens in the heat

April becomes May
sun darkens my skin
draws a light sweat
green brims the sky

Summer's Start

Light deepens the morning world.
June's early fire draws dawn before I wake.
It's cool before the dew burns off.
Mud in the ditch and leaves in the road
track the story of last night's storm.
The afternoon will be hot.

My house is shaded, coddled by woods
as I am coddled by solitude.
I love this world I once yearned to shed.
Dusk falls softly into the earth,
light drenches my reawakened life,
the massive star that is my heart.

Summer

a bath in early June air
brown arms, nape of neck burnt
night drive, black wind in my ears

lacking a lover I seek what loves me
I lose count
moss on rocks, dawn rushing the hill

fireflies spark up all my way home
I sleep and rise alone
not promised love, but summer

BIRTHING AGE

Elizabeth Nax

The grandmother visits the woman's sleep.
Her black wool skirt sweeps the floorboards.
Rickets totter her walk to the bed.
In death she has returned to the Old Country
but she never forgot her daughter's first child.
She smooths the quilt with work-rough hands,
she smooths the woman's hair,
loose on the pillow, hair white like her own.
She knows the eyes under the lids are her own blue.
In the lost language, she croons to her granddaughter,
now a grandmother herself.
Love flares in the sleeper's dream,
blue as a Sabbath candle flame,
warm as the kitchen of her grandmother's house.

Bathing Mama
for a grieving friend

To bathe Mama, in the hours following her last breath,
we daughters knelt by the tub to wash away the slight soil
of her dying weeks, obeying Mama's list of the last kindnesses
we could do her, as Daddy and our brothers waited
for tomorrow's work of burying.

Our washrags soaped her limbs,
loose in death which had been fitful in dying.
We kneeled side by side, each daughter knowing
she had been given her first basin bath by Mama,
who rested clean beneath our moving hands.

We toweled her dry without the power to hurt her,
admiring the lines of back, legs, arms, which could have been a bride's,
freed from the postures of pain which had lately shaped them.

The dress she had chosen was too wide;
her long fast had left only a younger woman's body.
Stockings, slip, dress, shoes, the rich hair twisted in a bun.

We daughters prepared our mother for her grave,
who had known in her last days to make us her handmaidens,
whose hands now lay quiet at her sides,
cupped in the form of a woman who shelters birds.

Down to a Point

At ninety-five, Frankie is so much as I knew her
when she was my teacher fifty years ago.
Her back is straight, her pale eyes flash and penetrate,
her laugh is deep and full.
But each time I leave her, after a too-brief visit,
I leave her too alone.
She tells me each time that more have gone.
The ranks of friends have thinned until
there are barely any left at all.
Lunch alone, dinner alone, walks alone, alone.
One's life, which was so crowded,
is narrowed down to a point.
She is always teaching me,
this woman who made me a teacher,
and I am learning once again.
She blows a kiss as I walk away,
as she always does, as she always will.

World
> *Another world is not only possible, she is on her way.*
> *On a quiet day, I can hear her breathing.*   ~Arundhati Roy

There's an echo, the in and out of breath
which fills each human, each animal ear,
stirs every blade of grass and every single leaf.
The planet, as it turns, is breathing.
She fills her lungs with empty air and lets it go.
Earth changes with each spin, each in and out.
Every animal, every human knows,
each blade of grass and leaf, down to its veins,
has an inkling of the echo of the dawn of change.
Listen to her.

Birthing Age

is not painless
there are scars
bloody losses

it's slow labor
easy to ignore
years long

unlike the brutal
hours
of birthing life

slick slippery
raging
with need

I grow pregnant
in ripe years
ready for release

give me strength
to lie down
bear down

birth this woman
bear forth
her good news

Joan Barasovska was born and grew up in Philadelphia. She has spent nearly half her life in the South, first in New Orleans, and for the last fifteen years in a rural area near Chapel Hill, North Carolina. Her undergraduate degree in Adult Education is from Antioch University and her M.Ed. in Psycho-Educational Processes is from Temple University. Joan is an academic therapist in private practice, working with children with learning disabilities and emotional and behavioral challenges. She cohosts a monthly poetry reading series in Chapel Hill and serves on the board of the North Carolina Poetry Society. She has written poems since childhood. Though she has published two instructional books for literacy teachers, *Birthing Age* is her first book of poetry. Joan has a daughter, a son, a stepson, and two grandsons.

www.ingramcontent.com/pod-product-compliance
Lightning Source LLC
LaVergne TN
LVHW041506070426
835507LV00012B/1359